The Old Old Story
Set to
Old Old Tunes

Katheryn Maddox Haddad

Katheryn Maddox Haddad

Northern Lights Publishing House

Copyright ©2015 by Katheryn Maddox Haddad
ISBN: 9781952261144

Printed in the United States

The Old Old Story Set to Old Old Tunes

Other Books By this Author For All Ages
A Child's Life of Christ: Set of 8
A Child's Bible Kids-Set of 8
A Child's Bible Heroes - Set of 10

The Old Old Story Set to Old Old Tunes
40 songs for the Old Testament
40 songs for the New Testament
All Set to Common Folk Tunes

Bible Puzzles for Young and Old
Secret Code, Crossword
Fill-in-the-Blank, Word Search

Fun With Bible Numbers
500 Arithmetic Problems Covering
Every Book in the Bible

Applied Christianity
A Handbook of 500 Good Works

Easy Bible Workbooks
Life of Christ According to Matthew
Acts of the Apostles
Letters of the Apostles-Part I & II
Old Testament Survey

iii

Katheryn Maddox Haddad
Table of Contents

OTHER BOOKS BY THIS AUTHOR FOR ALL AGES III

TABLE OF CONTENTS IV

OLD TESTAMENT 1
ADAM & EVE – SAMUEL 1
   1 ~ SIX DAYS OF CREATION 2
   2 ~ ADAM AND EVE 4
   3 ~ CAIN AND ABEL 5
   4 ~ ENOCH 5
   5 ~ METHUSELAH 6
   6 ~ NOAH 6
   7 ~ TOWER OF BABEL 7
   8 ~ JOB 8
   9 ~ SODOM AND GOMORRAH 9
   10 ~ ABRAHAM AND SARAH 10
   11 ~ Isaac 11
   12 ~ ESAU 11
   13 ~ JACOB 12
   14 ~ EGYPTIAN SLAVERY 13
   15 ~ MOSES 14
   16 ~ RAHAB 17
   17 ~ JOSHUA 17
   18 ~ GIDEON 18
   19 ~ SAMSON 19
   20 ~ SAMUEL 20

OLD TESTAMENT 23
RUTH – EZRA-NEHEMIAH 23
   21 ~ RUTH 24
   22 ~ SAUL, DAVID AND SOLOMON 24
   23 ~ SAUL 24
   24 ~ DAVID AND GOLIATH 25
   25 ~ ABSALOM 25
   26 ~ SOLOMON 26

The Old Old Story Set to Old Old Tunes

27 ~ JERABOAM AND REHABOAM 27
28 ~ ELIJAH 27
29 ~ ELISHA 30
30 ~ JONAH 31
31 ~ ISAIAH 32
32 ~ HEZEKIAH 33
33 ~ JOSIAH 34
34 ~ JEREMIAH 35
35 ~ TWELVE MINOR PROPHETS 35
36 ~ NEBUCHADNEZZAR 36
37 ~ SHADRACH, MESHAK, AND ABEDNEGO 37
38 ~ DANIEL 38
40 ~ EZRA AND NEHEMIAH 39

NEW TESTAMENT 40
LIFE OF JESUS 40
   41 ~ JESUS IS BORN 41
   42 ~ JESUS SEEN BY ANNA AND SIMEON 41
   43 - JESUS VISITS TEMPLE AT 12 42
   44 ~ JESUS' BAPTISM 42
   45 ~ JESUS' TEMPTATION 43
   46 ~ PARALYTIC LOWERED THROUGH ROOF 44
   47 ~ JESUS CALMS THE STORM 45
   48 ~ TWELVE APOSTLES 45
   49 ~ JOHN THE BAPTIST BEHEADED 46
   50 ~ JESUS FEEDS 5000 FAMILIES 47
   51 ~ JESUS WALKS ON THE SEA 48
   53 ~ JESUS' TRANSFIGURATION 49
   53 ~ THE PRODIGAL SON 49
   54 ~ LAZARUS 50
   55 ~ RICH MAN AND LAZARUS 51
   56 ~ TEN HEALED LEPERS 51
   57 ~ ZACCHAEUS 52
   58 ~ THE WIDOW AND HER MITE 53
   59 ~ JESUS' DEATH AND RESURRECTION 53
   60 ~ JESUS' ASCENSION TO HEAVEN 54

NEW TESTAMENT 55

THE CHURCH BEGINS.. 55
   61 ~ BIRTH OF THE CHURCH... 56
   62 ~ LORD'S SUPPER/COMMUNION 56
   63 ~ ANANIAS AND SAPPHIRA 57
   64 ~ STEPHEN... 57
   65 ~ ETHIOPIAN EUNUCH 58
   66 ~ CONVERSION OF SAUL/PAUL 59
   67 ~ DORCUS.. 60
   68 ~ CORNELIUS 61
   69 ~ PETER FREED FROM PRISON 62
   70 ~ PAUL'S MISSIONARY JOURNEYS 63
   71 ~ TIMOTHY 65
   72 ~ TITUS 66
   73 ~ WAY, TRUTH, LIFE 66
   74 ~ GOD IS FOR US 67
   75 ~ CHRISTIAN STRENGTH 67
   76 ~ CHRISTIAN LIVING 68
   77 ~ GOD'S GIFTS.. 68
   78 ~ GOD IS LOVE 69
   79 ~ VISION OF HEAVEN 69
   80 ~ RETURN OF JESUS 70

THANK YOU 71
ABOUT KATHERYN MADDOX HADDAD.................................. 72

BUY YOUR NEXT CHILD'S BOOK NOW..................................... 73
CONNECT WITH THE AUTHOR 74

GET A FREE BOOK... 74
JOIN MY DREAM TEAM.. 74

OLD TESTAMENT
Adam & Eve – Samuel

Katheryn Maddox Haddad
1 ~ SIX DAYS OF CREATION
Genesis 1:1 - 2:3
Tune: The Twelve Days of Christmas

On the first day of creation
God made earth, sky, and light,
And said that it was good.

Chorus:
Earth, sky and light,
And said that it was good.

On the second day of creation
God made the firmament,
And said that it was good.

Chorus:
The firmament,
Earth, sky and light
And said that it was good.

On the third day of creation
God made veggies and fruit,
And said that it was good.

Chorus:
Veggies and fruit,
The firmament,
Earth, sky, and light,
And said that it was good.

On the fourth day of creation

The Old Old Story Set to Old Old Tunes

God made sun, moon, and stars,
And said that it was good.

Chorus:
Sun, moon, and stars,
Veggies and fruit,
The firmament,
Earth, sky, and light,
And said that it was good.

On the fifth day of creation
God made the birds and fish
And said that it was good.

Chorus:
The birds and fish
Sun, moon, and stars,
Veggies and fruit,
The firmament,
Earth, sky, and light,
And said that it was good.

On the sixth day of creation
God made creatures and man,
And said that it was good.

Chorus:
Creatures and man,
Birds and fish,
Sun, moon, and stars,
Veggies and fruit,

Katheryn Maddox Haddad
The firmament,
Earth, sky, and light,
And said that it was good.

On the seventh day God rested,
And sanctified this day,
And said that it was good.

2 ~ ADAM AND EVE
Genesis 2:8 - 3:24
Tune: Polly Wolly Doodle

Oh, Adam and Eve had a garden fair ~
Obey the Lord all the day.
But they ate forbidden fruit on Satan's dare ~
Obey the Lord all the day.

Chorus:
Fare thee well, fare thee well,
Fare thee well, beautiful Eden.
The Lord they disobeyed;
With their lives they paid ~
Obey the Lord all the day.

The Old Old Story Set to Old Old Tunes

3 ~ CAIN AND ABEL
Genesis 4:1-8
Tune: Heart and Soul

Abel and Cain made sacrifices twain.
Abel's was sheep, but Cain's was only grain.
Cain was vain;
By his hand Abel was slain.

4 ~ ENOCH
Genesis 5:21-24
Tune: He's Gone Away

He's gone away for to stay with God on high.
And he'll not be back though he did not even die.
He's known as Enoch. His faith was like a rock.
And now he's with his God so full of love.
Gone away, gone away, far above.

Katheryn Maddox Haddad

5 ~ METHUSELAH
Genesis 5:22-27
Tune: Sweet Betsy From Pike

Oh, don't you remember the oldest of men?
Was Noah's grandfather, and oh what a kin!
Nine hundred and sixty-nine years his life span.
His name was Methuselah. What an old man!

6 ~ NOAH
Genesis 6:9 - 9:17
Tune: Sailing, Sailing

Sailing, sailing Noah prepared to do,
When God told him He'd flood the world
Because sin grew and grew.
"You must build the Ark of Gopher wood.
And I'll save animals all kinds,
And everyone that's good!"

Building, building, Noah set hard to work
While relatives and friends stood by

The Old Old Story Set to Old Old Tunes

To chuckle, laugh and smirk.
When the rains came and God closed up the gate,
There was Noah, Shem, Ham, Japheth,
And their wives, only eight.

Raining, raining forty long nights and days
Over the cities, trees and hills
The flood did raise and raise.
Finally the ark stopped on Ararat so high.
When they got off they saw the earth
All fresh and clean and dry.

Rainbow, rainbow God put up in the sky.
It's red and yellow, blue, and green.
Noah wondered why.
Never again flood will destroy mankind.
The bow's our promise from the Lord;
He'll never change His mind.

7 ~ TOWER OF BABEL
Genesis 11:1-9
Tune: Streets of Loredo

As God was watching the people of Babel
To see what they were doing so able,
He spied a new tower so great and so tall;

Katheryn Maddox Haddad
It rose far above the city's wall.

To reach up to heaven was their ambition.
To reach up to heaven ~ impossible mission!
He made them begin speaking languages so odd.
You can only get there by your faith in God.

8 ~ JOB
Job 1 - 42
Tune: Oh Dear! What Can the Matter Be?

Oh, dear! What can the matter be?
Dear, dear? What can the matter be?
Oh, dear! What can the matter be?
Satan claims Job doesn't love God.

Oh, dear! What can the matter be?
Dear, dear! What can the matter be?
Oh, dear! What can the matter be?
Job lost his health, wealth, and kin.

Oh, dear! What can the matter be?
Dear, dear! What can the matter be?
Oh, dear! What can the matter be?
Job's friends blame it on his sins.

Oh, dear! Why is Job happy?

The Old Old Story Set to Old Old Tunes

Dear, dear! Why is Job happy?
Oh, dear! Why is Job happy?
He loves God anyway.

Oh, dear! Why is Job happy?
Dear, dear! Why is Job happy?
Oh, dear! Why is Job happy?
Satan has left Job alone.

Oh, dear! Why is Job happy?
Dear, dear! Why is Job happy?
Oh, dear! Why is Job happy?
Job gained new health, wealth, and kin.

9 ~ SODOM AND GOMORRAH
Genesis 18:20 - 19:28
Tune: Scotland's Burning

Sodom and Gomorrah's burning, burning!
Repent! Repent!
Too late! Too late!
What upheaval! They were evil!

Katheryn Maddox Haddad

10 ~ ABRAHAM AND SARAH
Genesis 21:1-5
Tune: The Old Gray Mare

Abraham, Abraham, he ain't what he used to be,
Ain't what he used to be, ain't what he used to be.
Abraham, Abraham, he ain't what he used to be
Many long years ago.

Sarah, Sarah, she ain't what she used to be.
Ain't what she used to be, ain't what he used to be.
Sarah, Sarah, she ain't what she used to be
Many long years ago.

But God told them they'd have a little baby son,
Have a little baby son, have a little baby son,
Even though they'd never, ever had a son
Many long years before.

Sarah, Sarah, she is now ninety years of age,
Ninety years of age, ninety years of age.
Abraham, Abraham, he is a hundred years of age;
Too many long years of age.

Isaac, Isaac, they had their baby anyway,
Had their baby anyway, had their baby anyway.
Isaac, Isaac, they had their baby anyway

The Old Old Story Set to Old Old Tunes

When they were very old.

They're not so lonely like they used to be,
Like they used to be, like they used to be.
They're not so lonely like they used to be
'Cause God gave them a son.

11 ~ *Isaac*
Genesis 22:1-14
Tune: The Blue Bells of Scotland

"Oh where, oh where is the lamb to sacrifice?"
"The Lord will provide," Abe told Isaac so nice.
But when the altar was done,
'Twas Abraham's very own son.
Then the Lord stopped the knife,
And gave a ram for Isaac's life.

12 ~ *ESAU*
Genesis 25:29-34
Tune: A Tisket, A Tasket

Katheryn Maddox Haddad

Pottage, pottage, my birthright
for some pottage.
Esau sold his birthright to
Jacob for some pottage.

13 ~ JACOB
Genesis 37:1 - 46:30
Tune: Jolly Old St. Nicholas

Jolly old Jacob had a dozen sons:
Reuben, Simeon, Levi, Judah;
Dan, Naphtali, Gad and Asher;
Issachar, Zebulun, Joseph, Benjamin.

Joseph was his favorite. His brothers envied him,
Especially when he got a coat so colorful and trim.
And when he dreamed they'd bow to him.
Joseph they would slay;
Instead sold him as a slave
In Egypt far away.

Jolly old Jacob's not jolly anymore.
They claimed that Joseph had been slain,
"He's gone forever more."
The years passed by and he grew old,
His sadness was so great.

The Old Old Story Set to Old Old Tunes

But God watched over Joseph,
And happy was his fate.

A famine came to all the land
And Jacob's sons were weak.
They went to Egypt for some food.
To Joseph they bowed meek.
When they learned who he was,
Their father they did tell.
Then Jacob was so jolly again,
His heart rang like a bell.

14 ~ EGYPTIAN SLAVERY
Exodus 1:7-14
Tune: Yolga Boatmen's Song

Yo heave ho! (Ugh!) Yo heave ho! (Ugh!)
Make these bricks faster, make them faster!

Yo heaven ho! (Ugh!) Yo heave ho! (Ugh)
Build those cities high, for old Egypt!

Yo heave ho! (Ugh!) Yo heave ho! (Ugh!)
Slaves so long we've been, let us go!

Yo heave ho! (Ugh!) Yo heave ho! (Ugh)

Katheryn Maddox Haddad

15 ~ MOSES
Exodus 2 - Deuteronomy 34
Tune: Found a Peanut

Found Moses, found Moses,
Found Moses ~ the Bible says.
Pharaoh's daughter found Moses,
Found Moses ~ the Bible says.

Raised him as her son, raised him as her son,
Raised him as her son ~ the Bible says.
Pharaoh's daughter raised him as her son,
Raised him as her son ~ the Bible says.

Forty years a prince, forty years a prince,
Forty years a prince ~ the Bible says.
Forty years was an Egyptian prince,
An Egyptian prince ~ the Bible says.

Ran for his life, ran for his life,
Ran for his life ~ the Bible says.
Moses ran from Egypt for his life,
Ran for his life ~ the Bible says.

In the wilderness, in the wilderness,
In the wilderness ~ the Bible says.

The Old Old Story Set to Old Old Tunes

Forty years was in the wilderness,
In the wilderness ~ the Bible says.

Saw a burning bush, saw a burning bush,
Saw a burning bush ~ the Bible says.
Moses saw a holy burning bush,
Saw a burning bush ~ the Bible says.

Warned Pharaoh, warned Pharaoh,
Warned Pharaoh ~ the Bible says.
Warned Pharaoh to free the Israelites,
Free the Israelites ~ the Bible says.

Pharaoh wouldn't, Pharaoh wouldn't,
Pharaoh wouldn't ~ the Bible says.
Pharaoh wouldn't free the Israelites,
Free the Israelites ~ the Bible says.

God ten plagues, got ten plagues,
Got ten plagues ~ the Bible says.
Stubborn Egypt got ten plagues,
Got ten plagues ~ the Bible says.

Freed the Israelites, freed the Israelites,
Freed the Israelites ~ the Bible says.
Pharaoh finally freed the Israelites,
Freed the Israelites ~ the Bible says.

Crossed the Red Sea, crossed the Red Sea,
Crossed the Red Sea ~ the Bible says.
On dry land they crossed the Red Sea,

Katheryn Maddox Haddad
Crossed the Red Sea ~ the Bible says.

Quails and manna, quails and manna,
Quails and manna ~ the Bible says,
The Israelites ate quails and manna,
Quails and manna ~ the Bible says.

Ten Commandments, Ten Commandments,
Ten Commandments ~ the Bible says.
God gave them the Ten Commandments,
Ten Commandments ~ the Bible says.

Feared the Canaanites, feared the Canaanites,
Feared the Canaanites ~ the Bible says.
The Israelites feared the Canaanites,
Feared the Canaanites ~ the Bible says.

Wandered forty years, wandered forty years,
Wandered forty years ~ the Bible says.
The Israelites wandered forty years,
Wandered forty years ~ the Bible says.

Moses died, Moses died,
Moses died ~ the Bible says.
On Mt. Nebo Moses died,
Moses died ~ the Bible says.

The Old Old Story Set to Old Old Tunes

16 ~ RAHAB
Joshua 2:1-22
Tune: Blow the Man Down

Oh, let the spies down, Rahab,
Let the spies down
On the cord.
They're Israelites.

So, let the spies down, Rahab,
Let the spies down
Through your window.
Oh, let the spies down.

17 ~ JOSHUA
Joshua 6:1-27; 10:6-14
Tune: Skip to My Lou

Joshua marched around Jericho,
Joshua marched around Jericho,
Joshua marched around Jericho,
The Israelites did follow.

The people watched them seven days,
The people watched them seven days,
The people watched them seven days,

Katheryn Maddox Haddad
Laughing at such strange ways.

But evil was within that wall,
But evil was within that wall,
But evil was within that wall,
So God made it crumble and fall.

Joshua for the Gibeonites did fight,
Joshua for the Gibeonites did fight,
Joshua for the Gibeonites did fight,
But could not continue that night.

So God made the sun stand still and shine,
So God made the sun stand still and shine,
So God made the sun stand still and shine,
And they won the battle fine.

18 ~ GIDEON
Judges 7:1-23
Tune: Our Boys Will Shine

God's men will shine tonight, God's men will shine.
God's men will shine tonight, God's men will shine.
God's men will shine tonight, God's men will shine.
When the sun goes down and the moon comes up
God's men will shine.

The Old Old Story Set to Old Old Tunes

Thirty-two thousand men battle plans made.
"Too many men," God said, ten thousand stayed.
"Too many men still here with too much might!
They will boast that by their own strength they won
Such a great fight."

Three hundred men with horns, pitchers, and lights,
Ready to fight thousands of Midianites.
They blew their horns and toward them they did run.
Loud and clear they shouted, "The sword of the Lord,
And Gideon!"

The Midianites ~ you should have seen them go!
They knew the Lord God was their greatest foe.
God's men did shine tonight, God's men did shine.
When the sun went down and the moon came up,
God's men did shine!

19 ~ SAMSON
Judges 16:1-20
Tune: Where Is My Little Dog Gone?

Oh where, oh where have my muscles gone?
Oh where, oh where can they be?
With my own bare hands I have slain lions,
And Philistines numerously.

Katheryn Maddox Haddad

Oh where, oh where have my muscles gone?
Oh where, oh where can they be?
Gaza's gates I took to the top of a hill,
Don't bother with an old key.

Oh where, oh where have my muscles gone?
Oh where, oh where can they be?
My hair was the secret of my strength.
Delilah cut it! Poor me!

20 ~ SAMUEL
I Samuel 1:1 - 17:13
Tune: When I Was a Lady

When Samuel wasn't even born,
Wasn't even born, wasn't even born,
When Samuel wasn't even born
Hannah prayed for a son.

Chorus:
And this way she prayed [hands folded]
And that way she prayed.
When Samuel wasn't even born
Hannah prayed for a son.

When Samuel was a little boy,

The Old Old Story Set to Old Old Tunes

A little boy, a little boy,
When Samuel was a little boy
Hannah gave him to God.

Chorus:
And this way she gave him [hands outstretched]
And that way she gave him.
When Samuel was a little boy
Hannah gave him to God.

When Samuel was a big boy,
A big boy, a big boy,
When Samuel was a big boy
He heard the Lord call.

Chorus:
And this way he heard Him [cup ear]
And that way he heard him.
When Samuel was a big boy
He heard the Lord call.

When Samuel was a young man,
A young man, a young man,
When Samuel was a young man
He was prophet, judge, and priest.

Chorus:
And this way he taught men [cup mouth]
And that way he taught men.
When Samuel was a young man
He was prophet, judge, and priest.

Katheryn Maddox Haddad

When Samuel was an old man,
An old man, an old man,
When Samuel was an old man
He anointed Saul the king.

Chorus:
And this way anointed him [pour]
And that way anointed him.
When Samuel was an old man
He anointed Saul the king.

When Samuel was an ancient man,
An ancient man, an ancient man,
When Samuel was an ancient man
He anointed David king.

Chorus:
And this way anointed him [pour]
And that way anointed him.
When Samuel was an ancient man,
He anointed David king.

The Old Old Story Set to Old Old Tunes

OLD TESTAMENT

Ruth – Ezra-Nehemiah

Katheryn Maddox Haddad

21 ~ RUTH
Ruth 1-22
Tune: Home on the Range

Oh give Ruth a home where the Israelites roam,
Where they're good and righteous and pray;
Where often is heard the Lord God's holy Word,
And His love is more wondrous each day.

22 ~ SAUL, DAVID AND SOLOMON
I Samuel 9 - I Kings 22
Tune: Three Blind Mice

Three great kings, three great kings,
See how they ruled, see how they ruled.

Kings Saul, David and Solomon:
Their treasures were shining as the sun,
Fought many battles and many were won ~
Three great kings!

23 ~ SAUL

The Old Old Story Set to Old Old Tunes

I Samuel 9:15 - 13:7
Tune: Captain Jinks

I'm happily known by all as King Saul.
I am the very first king of Israel.
I used to be oh so shy and bashful,
But now I'm great and powerful!

24 ~ DAVID AND GOLIATH
I Samuel 17:1-58
Tune: Are You Sleeping?

Are you sleeping?
Are you sleeping?
Goliath? Goliath?

David's coming for you.
David's coming for you.
Goliath! Goliath!

25 ~ ABSALOM

Katheryn Maddox Haddad
II Samuel 18:9-17
Tune: Boll Weevil

Remember might Samson,
Oh Absalom, so fair.
You'll lose your life on a bad dare
Because of your long hair,
Because of your hair,
Because of your hair.

26 ~ SOLOMON
I Kings 3:5-7
Tune: Coming Through the Rye

Solomon built Jerusalem's walls
And his palace halls.
Then he built God's Temple grand ~
Most beautiful in the land.

Chorus:
Solomon was not selfish;
Chose wisdom as his wise
So he could lead his kingdom well ~
Got honor and riches as well.

The Old Old Story Set to Old Old Tunes

27 ~ JERABOAM AND REHABOAM
I Kings 12:1-20
Tune: Day is Done

Jeraboam, Rehaboam ~
You divided the Israel Kingdom.
Now it's two. Woe is you.
It's all through.

28 ~ ELIJAH
I Kings 17 - II Kings 2
Tune: Old McDonald Had a Farm

Elijah was a prophet of God,
A prophet of God was he.
He did what God commanded him
And so should you and me.

Chorus:
Love love here, love love there,

Katheryn Maddox Haddad
Here love, there love,
Everywhere love, love.
He did what God commanded him,
And so should you and me.

King Ahab was a wicked ole king;
Jezebel a wicked ole queen.
Elijah said there'll be no rain
And you'll be hungry and lean.

Chorus:
Thirsty here, thirsty there,
Here thirsty, there thirsty,
Everywhere thirsty,
Elijah said they'll be no rain
And you'll be hungry and lean.

But God hid Elijah in a cave
Beside a bubbling brook.
And ravens flew to him with food.
Thank God for each bite he took.

Chorus:
Thank you here, thank you there,
Here thank you, there thank you,
Everywhere thank you.
And ravens flew to him with food.
Thank God for each bite he took.

One day there was no more food to bring.
To a widow Elijah did god.
She shared the last of her meal and oil,

The Old Old Story Set to Old Old Tunes

And they forever did flow.

Chorus:
Oil oil here, oil oil there,
Here oil, there oil,
Everywhere oil, oil.
She shared the last of her meal and oil,
And they forever did flow.

The widow's son was very, very sick
And she was very, very sad.
But Elijah asked God to make him well.
Then everyone was very, very glad.

Chorus:
Gladness here, gladness there,
Here gladness, there gladness,
Everywhere gladness.
But Elijah asked God to make him well.
Then everyone was very, very glad.

Baal was made out of stone by men;
He was not a god at all.
But God sent fire right down from heaven
When He heard Elijah call.

Chorus:
Fire fire here, fire fire there,
Here fire, there fire,
Everywhere fire, fire.
But God sent fire right down from heaven

Katheryn Maddox Haddad
When He heard Elijah call.

At last the Lord called Elijah to come
'Cause his work on earth was done.
He rode to heaven in a chariot of fire
As shining as the sun.

Chorus:
Chariot here, chariot there,
Here chariot, there chariot,
Everywhere chariot.
He rode to heaven in a chariot of fire
As shining as the sun.

29 ~ ELISHA
II Kings 2 - 13
Tune: Pop Goes the Weasel

A Shunamite boy died one day,
And, oh, there was such sorrow.
Elisha raised him, and there was
Joy on the morrow.

Naaman suffered from leprosy.
Elisha's orders seemed silly.
Dipped seven times in muddy Jordan.
His skin was white as a lily.

The Old Old Story Set to Old Old Tunes

A famine came to all the land.
The Syrians came to conquer.
God made them hear an army so great;
They ran though no one was there.

30 ~ JONAH
Jonah 1 - 7
Tune: Farmer in the Dell

Jonah's in the fish!
Jonah's in the fish!
Jonah was afraid-ish,
Now Jonah's in the fish!

Jonah ran away!
Jonah ran away!
God's forgiveness he did pray
'Cause Jonah ran away!

Jonah got burped up!
Jonah got burped up!
Three days after being slurped up
Jonah got burped up!

To Nineveh he went!

Katheryn Maddox Haddad
To Nineveh he went!
Jonah caused them to repent
When to Nineveh he went!

31 ~ ISAIAH
Isaiah 1 - 66
Tune: The Campbells Are Coming

The Assyrians are coming. Beware! Beware!
The Assyrians are coming. Beware! Beware!
The Assyrians are coming to smash Jerusalem.
Isaiah warned them. Beware! Beware!

Jerusalem was saved, but beware! Beware!
Jerusalem was saved, but beware! Beware!
For Babylon will crush you right down to the ground.
Isaiah warned them. Beware! Beware!

King Cyrus will free you. O-ho! O-ho!
King Cyrus will free you. O-ho! O-ho!
King Cyrus will free you and rebuild Jerus'lem.
Isaiah told them. O-ho! O-ho!

King Jesus will save you. O-ha! O-ha!
King Jesus will save you. O-ha! O-ha!
King Jesus will save you in heaven so grand.
Isaiah told them. Oh-ho! O-ho!

The Old Old Story Set to Old Old Tunes

32 ~ HEZEKIAH
II Chronicles 29 - 32
Tune: Oh Susanna

Hezekiah was a righteous king,
The idols he tore down,
Opened up the long forgotten Temple
Where God's Word was found.

Chorus:
Hezekiah was a righteous king.
Opened up the long forgotten Temple
Where God's Word was found.

Hezekiah was a righteous king
The Assyrians came for war.
Then God's angel slew them in the night;
They tried it never more.

Chorus:
Hezekiah was a righteous king.
Then God's angel slew them in the night;
They tried it never more.

Hezekiah was a righteous king,

Katheryn Maddox Haddad
But one day almost died.
Fifteen years God added to his life
When to Him the king cried.

Chorus:
Hezekiah was a righteous king.
Fifteen years God added to his life
When to Him the king cried.

33 ~ JOSIAH
II Chronicles 34 - 35
Tune: Li'l Lisa Jane

Judah got a new king one great day: Josiah!
Just eight year old he was, by the way: Josiah!

Chorus:
King Josiah was his name.
King Josiah ~ great was his fame.

Sixteen years old looked for God above: Josiah!
So he could rule with King David's love: Josiah!

Chorus:
King Josiah was his name.
King Josiah ~ great was his fame.

The Old Old Story Set to Old Old Tunes

Twenty years old found God's Law long list: Josiah!
Down to the ground all idols he tossed: Josiah!

Chorus:
King Josiah was his name.
King Josiah ~ great was his fame.

34 ~ JEREMIAH
Jeremiah 1 - 52
Tune: The Last Rose of Summer

'Tis the last stand of Jerusalem,"
Jeremiah pleads. Oh, hear him.
"Tear your idols down, they're evil.
They're not gods, but the devil."

"The Lord is good; He'll save you.
Obey Him in all you do.
Do not let yourselves be destroyed.
Oh, be good and sin avoid."

35 ~ TWELVE MINOR PROPHETS

Katheryn Maddox Haddad
Hosea - Malachi
Tune: Twinkle, Twinkle Little Star

Hosea, Joel, Amos, Obadiah
Were four prophets of the Lord.
They warned Israel of their sin,
And to return to God again.
Hosea, Joel, Amos, Obadiah
Were four prophets of the Lord.

Jonah, Micah, Nahum, Habakkuk ~
Four more prophets of the Lord.
They warned Israel of their sin,
And to return to God again.
Jonah, Micah, Nahum, Habakkuk ~
Now there's eight prophets of the Lord.

Zephaniah, Haggai, Zechariah, Malachi ~
Four more prophets of the Lord.
They warned Israel of their sin,
And to return to God again.
Zephaniah, Haggai, Zechariah, Malachi ~
There's twelve minor prophets of the Lord.

36 ~ NEBUCHADNEZZAR
Daniel 1 - 3
Tune: London Bridge

The Old Old Story Set to Old Old Tunes

Jerusalem is falling down,
Falling down, falling down.
Jerusalem is falling down
To the ground.

Neb-bu-chad-nez-zar did it.
He did it, he did it.
Neb-bu-chad-nez-zar did it.
Every bit.

Took the Jews to Babylon,
Babylon, Babylon.
Took the Jews to Babylon.
That was no fun.

To his statue they must bow,
They must bow, they must bow.
To his statue they must bow ~
Wouldn't anyhow!

37 ~ SHADRACH, MESHAK, AND ABEDNEGO
Daniel 3:1-30
Tune: Clementine

Shadrach, Meshach and Abednego

Katheryn Maddox Haddad

Were three God-fearing men.
They refused to bow to any but God,
For that would have been sin.

Shadrach, Meshach and Abednego ~
In a furnace they were thrown.
But they did not even get burned,
For they were not alone.

God was with them, God was with them
In the furnace on that day.
Nebuchadnezzar believed in God,
For he learned that faith does pay.

38 ~ DANIEL
Daniel 6:1-23
Tune: Blue Tail Fly

The king commanded that for thirty days
Only he could grant favors or take praise.
But Daniel always prayed to God on high.
Was thrown in a lions' den to die.

Chorus:
Daniel the lions didn't slay.
Daniel the lions didn't slay.
Daniel the lions didn't slay.

The Old Old Story Set to Old Old Tunes

God was with him night and day.

40 ~ EZRA AND NEHEMIAH
Ezra 4 - 5; Nehemiah 2 - 6
Tune: Deck the Halls

Build the Temple up again.
Fa la la la la, la la la la.
Ezra wants to teach therein.
Fa la la la la, la la la la.

Chorus:
They've come back from Babylon.
For the Jews have returned to their land.
Build the Temple up again.
Ezra wants to teach therein.

Build the walls of Jerusalem higher.
Fa la la la la, la la la la.
Nehemiah will not tire.
Fa la la la la, la la la la.

Chorus:
They've come back from Babylon.
For the Jews have returned to their land.
Build the walls of Jerusalem higher.emiah will not tire.

Katheryn Maddox Haddad

NEW TESTAMENT
Life of Jesus

The Old Old Story Set to Old Old Tunes

41 ~ JESUS IS BORN
Luke 2:1-20
Tune: Mary Had a Little Lamb

Mary had a baby boy,
Baby boy, baby boy.
Mary had a baby boy.
His heart was pure and white.

Everywhere that Mary went,
Joseph went, Jesus went,
Everywhere their family went
God was sure to go.

42 ~ JESUS SEEN BY ANNA AND SIMEON
Luke 2:21-38
Tune: Rock-a-bye Baby

Rock-a-bye, Jesus, in Simeon's arms.
Go to sleep, Jesus, do not fear harms.
Simeon's so happy now he's seen You.
Old Anna's rejoicing; she's seen You too.

Katheryn Maddox Haddad

43 - JESUS VISITS TEMPLE AT 12
Luke 2:42-52
Tune: Yankee Doodle

Jesus went to Jerusalem, a riding on a burro
So he could visit the Temple of God.
He became all children's hero.

He knew the Scriptures very well,
And when He talked to the men there,
They were amazed that at only twelve
He had such wisdom rare.

44 ~ JESUS' BAPTISM
Matthew 3:13-17
Tune: Down in the Valley

Down in the Jordan River so blue
John the Baptist preached to lots of Jews.
Jesus came to him with a request.
"Will you baptize Me, like all the rest?"

The Old Old Story Set to Old Old Tunes

Down in the Jordan Jesus did go,
Under the water He went down low.
When He came up, to Him came a dove.
"This is My son," a Voice said above.

Down in the Jordan Jesus did give
Us an example of how to live.
We'll follow You, Lord, in all you do
So we can join You in heaven too.

45 ~ JESUS' TEMPTATION
Matthew 4:1-11
Tune: bury Me Not on the Lone Prairie

Oh listen not to the old devil!
He never is on the level.
He'll make you sin
Again and again!

Jesus had starved forty days and nights.
Satan told Him to prove his mights.
"Make bread of this stone." [Satan]
"Don't live by bread alone." [Jesus]

Satan took Him to a high mountain,
Said he'd give Him all under the sun.

Katheryn Maddox Haddad
"Only worship me." [Satan]
"God alone is holy." [Jesus]

Satan took Him on the Temple high.
"God shall not surely let You die,
Make a jumping attempt." [Satan]
"The Lord God never tempt." [Jesus]

46 ~ PARALYTIC LOWERED THROUGH ROOF
Mark 2:1-12
Tune: Mulberry Bush

Here we go 'round the great big crowd,
Great big crowd, great big crowd.
Here we go 'round the great big crowd,
Our entrance not allowed.

In the roof we'll make a slot,
Make a slot, make a slot.
In the roof we'll make a slot,
And lower the sick man's cot.

Look at Jesus make him stand,
Make him stand, make him stand.
Look at Jesus make him stand.
His miracle's so grand!

The Old Old Story Set to Old Old Tunes

47 ~ JESUS CALMS THE STORM
Matthew 8:23-27
Tune: Oh Christmas Tree

Oh Jesus, Lord! Oh Jesus, Lord!
The storm will throw us overboard.
Oh don't you care? Oh please wake up.
Our little boat will soon break up.
Oh Jesus, Lord! Oh Jesus, Lord!
The storm will throw us overboard.

"Where is your faith? Why do you fear?
For I am always with you here."
Then He commanded, "Peace, be still."
The winds and sea obeyed His will.
"Where is your faith? Why do you fear?
For I am always with you here."

48 ~ TWELVE APOSTLES
Matthew 10:2-4; Acts 2:1-8
Tune: Dashing Through the Snow

Katheryn Maddox Haddad

Peter, Andrew, James and John,
Philip and Bartholomew,
Thomas, Matthew, Thaddeus,
Simon, James and Judas.

[Repeat]

Chorus:
Twelve Apostles, Twelve Apostles
Chosen by the Lord.
For the work that they must do
The Holy Spirit was poured.

Twelve Apostles, Twelve Apostles
Chosen by the Lord.
Lived for Christ and died for him.
Heaven's their reward.

49 ~ JOHN THE BAPTIST BEHEADED
Matthew 14:1-12
Tune: In the Evening By the Moonlight

In the evening in the palace
You can hear the music playing;
While down in the dark old dungeon
John the Baptist is now praying.

The Old Old Story Set to Old Old Tunes

Herodius' daughter danced so grand
That her wish was Herod's command.
She wants the head of John the Baptist.

50 ~ JESUS FEEDS 5000 FAMILIES
Matthew 14:13-21
Tune: The Old Chisolm Trail

Well, listen everyone to what the Bible said.
It tells you of 5000 men Jesus fed.

Chorus:
Come-a-ti-yi youp-py, youp-py ya, youp-py ya!
Come-a-ti-yi youp-py, youp-py ya!

They follow Jesus to the desert bare and brown.
Suddenly got hungry, but not near a town.

Chorus:
Come-a-ti-yi youp-py, youp-py, youp-py ya!
Come-a-ti-yi youp-py, youp-py ya!

They found five little loaves, and fishes only two.
But Jesus said that they would surely do.

Chorus:

Katheryn Maddox Haddad
Come-a-ti-yi youp-py, youp-py, youp-py ya!
Come-a-ti-yi youp-py, youp-py ya!

He thanked the Lord, passed them out to everyone.
Gathered twelve full baskets when they were all done.

Chorus:
Come-a-ti-yi youp-py, youp-py, youp-py ya!
Come-a-tio-yi younp-py, youp-py ya!

51 ~ JESUS WALKS ON THE SEA
Matthew 14:22-33
Tune: My Bonnie

My Jesus walks on the water,
My Jesus walks on the sea,
My Jesus walks on the water.
Now Peter is trying, oh me.

Now Peter walks on the water,
Now Peter walks on the sea,
Now Peter walks on the water.
He's sinking, oh hear his plea.

Together they walk on the water,
Together they walk on the sea.
Together they walk on the water.

The Old Old Story Set to Old Old Tunes

Have faith in the Lord constantly.

53 ~ JESUS' TRANSFIGURATION
Luke 9:28-36
Tune: On Top of Old Smokey

On top of the mountain Jesus did go.
And while He was praying, like sun He did glow.

Then Moses, Elias appeared to Him there.
And as they were talking, Apostles did stare.

So Peter said, "Let's make tents for all three ~
One for Elias and Moses and Thee."

A bright cloud came down and covered up them.
"This is My loved Son, hear only Him!"

53 ~ THE PRODIGAL SON
Luke 15:11-24
Tune: The Girl I Left Behind Me

Katheryn Maddox Haddad

I was lonesome since my money was all gone;
Nobody liked me any more.
I was hungry and wished I could eat
Like I did at home before.

I finally went back home
And asked for the treatment of a servant.
But my father welcomed me as his son.
His love for me very fervent.

54 ~ LAZARUS
John 11:1-45
Tune: Arkansas Traveller

Mary and Martha were very sad,
For Lazarus had a sickness very bad.
To Jesus they did send the sad, sad word,
Hoping He would come as soon as He heard.

Lazarus died, and then Jesus came.
And in tears He called out Lazarus' name.
Though he'd been in the grave three days,
He rose up alive, to the crowd's amaze.

The Old Old Story Set to Old Old Tunes

55 ~ RICH MAN AND LAZARUS
Luke 16:19-31
Tune: Loch Lomon

By yon bonnie banks and by yon bonnie braes
Where the sun shines bright up in heaven.
Where Lazarus was taken, the rich man could not go ~
To the bonnie, bonnie banks up in heaven.

Chorus:
Oh the rich man was selfish,
Although he was wealthiest,
And poor Lazarus never got any.
Now he cannot have any water coolish,
'Cause his life on earth was sinful and foolish.

56 ~ TEN HEALED LEPERS
Luke 17:11-19
Tune: Ten Little Indian Boys

1 healed, 2 healed, 3 healed lepers,

Katheryn Maddox Haddad

4 healed, 5 healed, 6 healed lepers,
7 healed, 8 healed, 9 healed lepers ~
10 lepers healed by Christ.

10 healed, 9 healed, 8 healed lepers,
7 healed, 6 healed, 5 healed lepers,
4 healed, 3 healed, 2 healed lepers ~
1 leper stayed to thank Christ.

57 ~ ZACCHAEUS
Luke 19:1-10
Tune: Billy Boy

"Oh, where have you been, Zaccheus, Zaccheus?
Oh, where have you been, Zaccheus?"
"I've been in a Sycamore tree,
So my Lord I could see;
And He noticed so stopped to talk to me."

"Oh, who have you there, Zaccheus, Zaccheus?
Oh, who have you there, Zaccheus?"
"I tried so hard to see Him there
That He said, my home He'd share.
Even though I am short, He doesn't care."

The Old Old Story Set to Old Old Tunes

58 ~ THE WIDOW AND HER MITE
Luke 21:1-4
Tune: Goodnight, Ladies

Some gave millions, the widow gave one.
But hers was the greatest gift:
For herself she kept none.

Chorus:
When we give much top the Lord,
To the Lord, to the Lord,
When we give much to the Lord,
Much more is our reward.

59 ~ JESUS' DEATH AND RESURRECTION
John 19 - 20; Acts 1:1 - 11
Tune: Londonderry Air

Jesus died on the cross so I may live with Him.
He paid the price to free me from my sin.
After three days, He rose up from His garden grave

Katheryn Maddox Haddad
To show that He has power my soul to save.

He lived a life for me to follow every day.
He said He is the Truth, the Life, the Way.
He promised to return and then rose to the sky.
I know that I will join Him when I die.

60 ~ JESUS' ASCENSION TO HEAVEN
Acts 1:9-11
Tune: Hail! Hail! The Gang's All Here!

Hail! Hail! Jesus rose!
He has conquered our foes!
Watch the way His church grows!
Hail! Hail! Jesus rose!
See how far His great love flows

The Old Old Story Set to Old Old Tunes

NEW TESTAMENT

The Church Begins

Katheryn Maddox Haddad

61 ~ BIRTH OF THE CHURCH
Acts 2:1-47
Tune: Wearing of the Green

Oh, my friend dear, and did you hear
The news that's going 'round?
Jesus has risen, and His followers
Everywhere are found.

Oh, Peter preached the first sermon,
Said, "Live forever more,
If you will repent of your sins
And do them never more."

Oh, 3000 obeyed God's will
And were baptized that day.
And now they're telling everyone
Of Jesus' loving way.

62 ~ LORD'S SUPPER/COMMUNION
I Corinthians 11:23-28
Tune: Drink To Me Only With Thine Eyes

Re-mem-ber Jesus when you eat of the bread
That He rose up from the dead.

The Old Old Story Set to Old Old Tunes

And when you drink the fruit of the vine,
Of his blood it is a sign.

How happy to know that Jesus loved me
When He died on Calvary.

He took my place: Punished for my sins.
He's the greatest of my Friends.

63 ~ ANANIAS AND SAPPHIRA
Acts 5:1-10
Tune: Hickory Dickory Dock

Sapphira and Ananias
Got themselves in a muss.
To God they lied,
So then they died ~
Sapphira and Ananias.

64 ~ STEPHEN
Acts 7:54-60
Tune: What Child is This?

Katheryn Maddox Haddad
What man is this
Who'd die for Jesus?
Watch him moan
As him they stone.
He preached God's love to all men.
This Christian's name is Stephen.

65 ~ ETHIOPIAN EUNUCH
Acts 8:26-39
Tune: Froggie Went a Courtin'

Eunuch was a reading while he did ride.
Hmmmm, hmmmm.
Eunuch was a reading while he did ride
When by Philip he was spied.
Hmmmm, hmmmm.

Philip told him that the Savior came.
Hmmmm, hmmmm.
Philip told him that the Savior came
And that Jesus was His name.
Hmmmm, hmmmm.

The Eunuch said, "Please baptize me."
Hmmmm, hmmmm.
The Eunuch said, "Please baptize me,
So I can a Christian be."

The Old Old Story Set to Old Old Tunes

Hmmmm, hmmmm.

66 ~ CONVERSION OF SAUL/PAUL
Acts 9:1-31
Tune: Get Along Home, Cindy

Saul headed for Damascus so that
Christians he could find,
And persecute them everyone
If they wouldn't change their mind.

Chorus:
Get along, Saul, to the Christians,
Get along, Saul.
Get along, Saul, to the Christians,
And off to prison haul.

Saul headed for Damascus.
On the way a voice he heard.
He was blinded by the light
That glowed with Jesus' Word.

Chorus:
Get along, Saul, to the Christian,
Get along, Saul.
Get along, Saul, to the Christian,

Katheryn Maddox Haddad
For you have heard God's call.

Saul headed for Damascus.
Ananias said what to do.
He believed in Jesus, was baptized,
And became a Christian too.

Chorus:
Get along, Saul, to the Christians,
Get along, Saul.
Get along, Saul, to the Christians;
You'll love them after all.

Saul headed from Damascus.
to preach to all the earth
How Jesus died for everyone,
And of a new re-birth.

Chorus:
Get along, Saul, to the whole earth,
Get along, Saul.
Get along, Saul, to the whole earth;
And you'll now be called Paul.

67 ~ DORCUS
Acts 9:36-42
Tune: Sing a Song of Six Pence

The Old Old Story Set to Old Old Tunes

Sing a son of Dorcas, a pocket full of thread.
Sewed for the poor widows, then died on her bed.

Peter came unto her; to God he then did pray.
Dorcas was return to life the same hour of the day.

68 ~ CORNELIUS
Acts 10:1-48
Tune: First Noel

God spoke to Peter in a noon-time vision
And told him to go on a special mission.
Salvation is for all, not just the Jews.
The Gentiles can also receive the Good News.

Chorus:
Our Savior loves all people of every race.
He never holds back His loving grace.

Cor-ne-li-us was a cen-tur-ion,
And also a Gentile, so not a Christian.
Peter came to him and taught him Jesus.
The first Gentile Christian was Cor-ne-li-us.

Katheryn Maddox Haddad

Chorus:
Our Savior loves all people of every race.
He never holds back His loving grace.

69 ~ PETER FREED FROM PRISON
Acts 12:1-11
Tune: Buffalo Gals

Peter was preaching in Jerusalem,
Jerusalem, in Jerusalem
When he was taken to prison
So dark and damp and dim.

The Christians gathered and prayed for him,
Prayed for him, prayed for him;
For they feared that he would soon be slain ~
And, oh, how they'd miss him.

"Apostle Peter, won't you come out tonight?
Come out tonight, come out tonight?"
An angel was there and led him out.
Peter hardly believed his sight.

The Old Old Story Set to Old Old Tunes

70 ~ PAUL'S MISSIONARY JOURNEYS
Acts 13 - 28
Tune: A Roving, A Roving

To Cyprus Island Paul did go
So Jesus' love they'd know.
The governor believed Jesus.
The Word spread all through Cyprus.

Chorus:
Then Paul went on a roving to teach lost men.
A roving, a roving to teach God's word, their souls to win.
Then Paul went on a roving to teach lost men.

A Lystra town the lame was healed.
To Paul and Barabbas kneeled
As Jupiter and Mercury.
Told them not to, then had to flee.

Chorus

To Philippi a dream led Paul ~
The Macedonian call.
But in prison Paul was cast.
An earthquake released him at last.

Chorus

To Athens Paul did travel next.
The idols made him vexed.

Katheryn Maddox Haddad
He taught the people on Mars Hill,
But few obeyed God's holy will.

Chorus

At Corinth Paul lived over a year.
Priscilla, Aquila were near.
Crispus, a ruler of the Jews,
Believed, obeyed Jesus' Good News.

Chorus

In Ephesus two years Paul stayed.
In a school his teachings were made.
Magicians all their books did burn
When God's true Way they all did learn.

Chorus

To Troas Paul went later on.
Till midnight his sermon.
From a window a young man did fall,
But was brought back to life by Paul.

Chorus

To Jerusalem Paul returned at last,
Although his warnings were vast.
The Jews attempted him to slay.
The Romans took him safe away.

Chorus

The Old Old Story Set to Old Old Tunes

To Caesarea Paul then was sent.
Two years in jail he spent.
Felix, Festus, Agrippa he taught,
But wealth and power were all they sought.

Chorus

To Rome Paul went a captive.
In a house permitted to live.
Two years he waited for a trial.
Freely preached God's Word all the while.

Chorus

71 ~ TIMOTHY
II Timothy 1:1-6
Tune: Shortnin' Bread

Eunice' little boy loves Jesus, Jesus.
Lois' little grandson loves Jesus Lord.

Timothy's his name, he loves Jesus, Jesus.
He will grow up and teach Jesus' Word.

Katheryn Maddox Haddad

72 ~ TITUS
Titus 1:1-5
Tune: Paper of Pins

Oh, Titus was a young Grecian man
Who taught the Lord's salvation plan.
He traveled much with Paul.
Was peaceful and loving to all.

73 ~ WAY, TRUTH, LIFE
John 14:6a
Tune: Oh, How Lovely Is the Evening

I am the Way, the Truth, the Life,
Way, the Truth, the Life.

I am the Way, the Truth, the Life,
Way, the Truth, the Life.

John fourteen, six.
John fourteen, six.

The Old Old Story Set to Old Old Tunes

74 ~ GOD IS FOR US
Romans 8:31
Tune: Pawpaw Patch

If God is for us, who can be against us?
If God is for us, who can be against us?
If God is for us, who can be against us?
Romans eight, thirty-one.

75 ~ CHRISTIAN STRENGTH
Philippians 4:13
Tune: Darling Nellie Gray

"I can do all things through Jesus Christ
who strengthens me,"
Says Paul in Philippians four, thirteen.

"I can do all things through Jesus Christ
who strengthens me,"
Says Paul in Philippians four, thirteen.

Katheryn Maddox Haddad

76 ~ CHRISTIAN LIVING
Colossians 3:17
Tune: Vesper Hymn

"Whatever you do in word or in deed
Do all in the name of Jesus Christ,
Giving thanks to God, the Father, by Him,"
Wrote Paul in Colossians three, verse seventeen.

77 ~ GOD'S GIFTS
James 1:17a
Tune: My Pony

Every good gift comes from God above,
Every good gift comes from God above,
Every good gift comes from God above,

Every good gift comes from God above,
Every good gift comes from God above,
James one, seventeen read.
Good meets all our needs.

The Old Old Story Set to Old Old Tunes

78 ~ GOD IS LOVE
I John 4:8
Tune: Good Christian Men, Rejoice

All men and women, girls and boys
Fill your heart with joys.
For we know that God is love. Love! Love!
See God's Word, first John four, eight.
His love we appreciate!

79 ~ VISION OF HEAVEN
Revelation 21:10-27
Tune: Juanita

Heaven is beau-ti-ful
With twelve gates of finest pearl.
Diamond is its wall,
So great and tall.

In bright sparkling tones
Glow the twelve foundation stones.

Katheryn Maddox Haddad
And the streets are gold.
Christians will behold...

Chorus:
...heaven, beautiful heaven,
Where God's throne in splendor stands.
Heaven, beautiful heaven.
God holds out His hands.

80 ~ RETURN OF JESUS
Revelation 22:12-14
Tune: Angels We Have Heard on High

Jesus I will see up high
Coming right down from the sky.
And if I've been true to Him,
He will take me home to heaven.

Chorus:
Glo-o-o-ria!
He will come for me.
Glo-o-o-ria!
Then at last God's face I'll see.

THANK YOU

Thanks for reading my book! I'm so honored that you entrusted me with your child and chose to spend your precious time together with my book. You are appreciated.

I'm an independent author who relies on my readers to help spread the word about stories you enjoy. Would you take a few minutes to let your friends know on Facebook, Pinterest... wherever you hang out online?

Also, each honest review at online retailers means a lot to me and helps other readers know if this is a book they might enjoy.

I welcome contact from readers. At my website (below), you can do so. You can also sign up for my newsletter (below) to be notified of half-price books for the whole family and new releases.

•

Katheryn Maddox Haddad
About Katheryn Maddox Haddad

Katheryn Maddox Haddad grew up in the north and now lives in Arizona where she doesn't have to shovel sunshine. She basks in 100-degree weather with palm trees, cacti, and a computer with most of the letters worn off.

Her children's books are most popular among grandparents and home schoolers. But they are popular with children around the world. Her many novels and information books are popular with the grownups.

Her newspaper column appeared in newspapers in Texas and North Carolina—*Little Known Facts About the Bible*.

She spends half her day writing, and the other half teaching English over the internet worldwide using the Bible as text book. Students she has converted to Christianity are in hiding all over the Middle East. "They are my heroes," she declares.

Each morning she sends out an inspirational scripture thought to over 30,000 people worldwide.

She is a member of American Christian Fiction Writers and International Screenwriters Association.

The Old Old Story Set to Old Old Tunes

Buy Your Next Child's Book Now

.A CHILD'S LIFE OF CHRIST Series of 8 books
- http://bit.ly/ChildsLifeOfChristSet

A CHILD'S BIBLE HEROES Series of 10 books
http://bit.ly/ChildBibleHeroes

A CHILD'S BIBLE KIDS Series of 8 books
40 from O.T. 40 from N.T.
http://bit.ly/ChildsParables

OLD OLD STORY SET TO OLD OLD TUNES
http://bit.ly/BibleSongBook

FUN WITH BIBLE NUMBERS: 525 Problems
http://bit.ly/FunBibleNumbers

BIBLE PUZZLES FOR YOUNG & OLD
http://bit.ly/BiblePuzzlesYoungOld

APPLIED CHRISTIANITY:
A HANDBOOK OF 500 GOOD WORKS.
http://bit.ly/500GoodWorks

EASY BIBLE WORKBOOKS
Life of Christ According to Matthew
Acts of the Apostles
Letters of the Apostles-Part I & II
Old Testament Survey
https://bit.ly/3fKdVFB

Katheryn Maddox Haddad

CONNECT WITH THE AUTHOR

Website: https://inspirationsbykatheryn.com
Facebook: bit.ly/FacebooksKatherynMaddoxHaddad
Linkedin: http://bit.ly/KatherynLinkedin
Twitter: https://twitter.com/KatherynHaddad
Pinterest: https://www.pinterest.com/haddad1940/
Goodreads:
 https://www.goodreads.com/katherynmaddoxhaddad

GET A FREE BOOK

Sign up for Katheryn's monthly newsletter with half-price books for the whole family and insider tips on what's coming next .   http://bit.ly/katheryn

JOIN MY DREAM TEAM

Members get the first peak at my newest book and have fun offering me advice sometimes. I have a point system of rewards for helping me get the word out. Check it out here: http://bit.ly/KatherynsDreamTeam